CW00406011

Cooking with Scorsese
and others

Volume 2

Hato Press

Contents

Preface

Spending time between the covers of Cooking with Scorcese brings to mind the Wallace Stevens poem <u>Thirteen Ways of Looking at a Blackbird</u>.

Without delving into graduate-school thought-talk about the ontological or non-ontological functions of either, what they do on their surface — and, hey, I'm a food writer, so surface is really the depth at which I'm most comfortable — is they invite us to look and think and consider, to piece together the still frames (or bare lines) into a moving image in our minds' eyes and find our connection to it.

The cooking in Scorcese's movies functions this way. When I was little I thought of them as some part of my Italian-American heritage, and watching those scenes felt like stolen moments of intimacy, a chance to see how men who otherwise spoke of guns and power and revenge (or, closer to home, children, debt, and work) related to each other outside of their publically masculine personae.

Over time, I realised there is a masculinity, a power dynamic to this cooking, the transfer

of knowledge between cook and onlooker:
'this is the way to do it, this is the way we do it.'
As a teenager that felt powerful to me; something
to aspire to. It was cooking where the exclusion
of not knowing played a key part in the cooks'
self-definition. I now think of that as a trait
common among young cooks and chefs in the
restaurant business.

With age, though, we see the fallacy of that kind
of thinking. Imagine <u>Goodfellas</u>, when Ray
Liotta's Henry Hill admonishes his wheelchair-
bound brother Mikey about the importance of
stirring the sauce even as the police helicopters
are closing in and his world is about to collapse
on him. It's about holding on to choice traditions
of the culture that had otherwise largely failed
them, about controlling the littlest things even as
the big ones have slipped away.

This is what those scenes from this one director
have meant to me, and they may not have meant
those things to you: maybe Liotta's voice just tells
you to make sure the garlic is cut thinly enough
that it will liquefy in the pan.

But that is the magic of this book. Here are the
scenes from a dozen-plus movies, snipped out
of context, snatched off the silver screen and laid
out in an orderly fashion so we can experience

them out of time, on our own. In some cases they may provoke a sort of decontextualized reconsideration of scenes you already know ('I never thought about it that way'), they may offer a point-of-entry to a film, or a filmmakers work you've never known ('I want to see the movie where they cook that').

The magic is that it doesn't tell you what to think or how to think or what the filmmaker behind the scenes was thinking. The magic is that it says this: look, and think for yourself.

— Peter Meehan, Editor, <u>Lucky Peach</u>

Cooking with Scorsese and Others Volume 3
will be coming soon. To suggest any films to be
included please email: scorsese@hatopress.net.

The following movies are set to be included:

301/302
A Touch of Spice
Benny and Joon
Estômago – A Gastronomic Story
Happy Together
In the Mood for Love
Julie and Julia
Like Water for Chocolate
Porco Rosso
Scent Of Green Papaya
Tampopo
Taxi Driver
The Chef of the South Polar
The Godfather
The Grande Bouffe and Blow-Out
The Night Porter
Today's Special
Zazie in the Metro

You're not eating
much, sonny.
Can I fix you
something?
... A rice omelet.

Jûzô Itami
<u>Tampopo</u> (1985)

You're not eating much, sonny.
Can I fix you something?

- A rice omelet.
- Rice omelet. Hmm.

Okay, follow me.

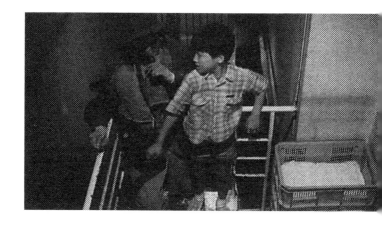

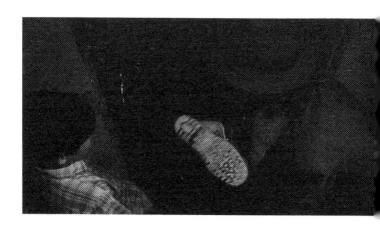

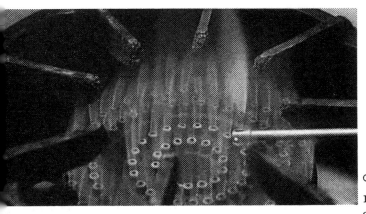

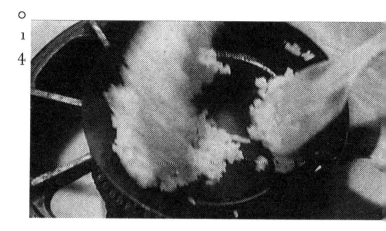

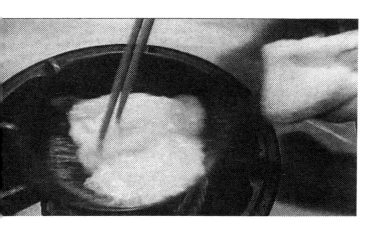

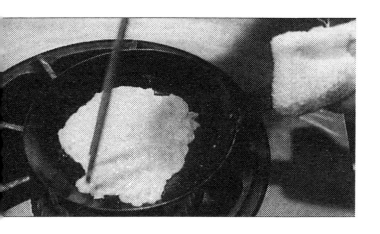

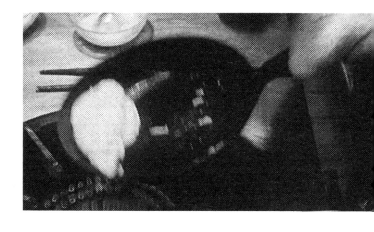

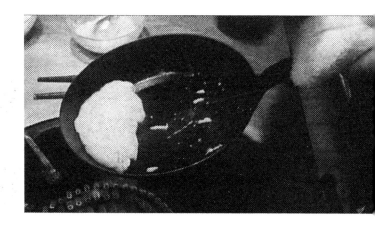

[Handmade ramen noodle]

Shûichi Okita
The Chef of the South Polar (2009

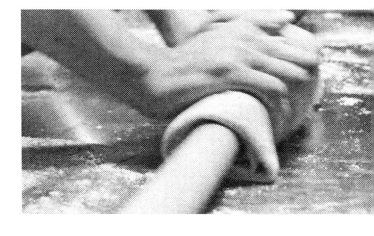

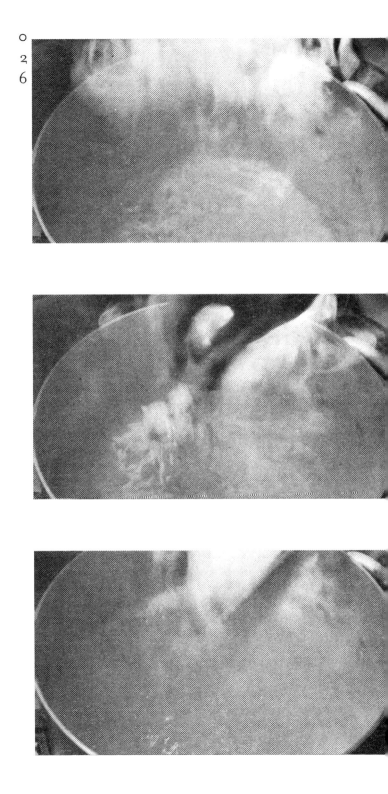

[Ramen toppings]

Jûzô Itami
<u>Tampopo</u> (1985)

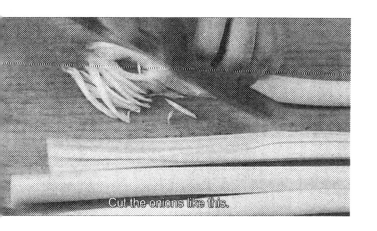

Cut the onions like this.

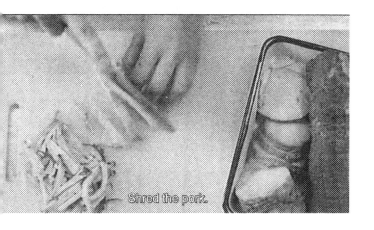

Shred the pork.

Fry them lightly, put them on
the noodles. Add a dash of sesame oil.

STEPS
I- The Pastry
II- The Filling
III- The Decoration
IV- The Assembly

Wes Anderson
Grand Budapest Hotel (2014)

HOW TO MAKE
MENDL'S
COURTESAN AU CHOCOLAT

STEPS

I-   THE PASTRY
II- THE FILLING
III- THE DECORATION
IV- THE ASSEMBLY

I- THE PASTRY

Make a choux pastry of flour,
water, butter and eggs.

Though correct proportions
may vary depending on one's
elevation and humidity, we
recommend:

1 cup plain flour
1 cup fresh water
1/4lb butter
4 eggs beaten in a bowl
A pinch of salt
A larger pinch of sugar

Bring the water, butter, salt and sugar to a boil.

Bring the water, butter, salt and sugar to a boil.

Remove from the fire and quickly mix in the sifted flour.

Return to heat for a few minutes, stirring, and cook until the dough forms a single lump.

Allow to cool just enough to keep the eggs from cooking and stir in very gradually with a strong wooden spoon.

Allow to cool just enough to keep the eggs from cooking and stir in very gradually with a strong wooden spoon.

Pipe the dough into small, medium and large-size dollops on a tray.

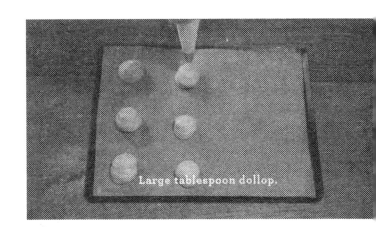

Large tablespoon dollop.

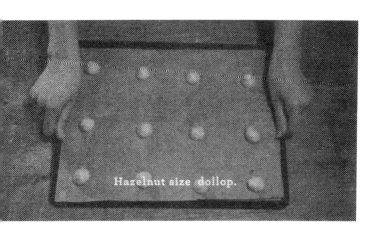

Hazelnut size dollop.

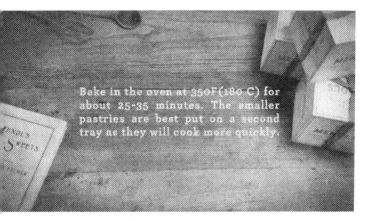

Bake in the oven at 350F(180 C) for about 25-35 minutes. The smaller pastries are best put on a second tray as they will cook more quickly.

Remove from the oven and discretely make a small piercing in the choux to allow the steam to escape.

II- THE FILLING

Once cooled, the large and medium choux should be filled with a creme pâtissière of chocolate, egg yolks, and sugar.

1 1/2 cups whole milk
Several large pieces semi-sweet chocolate
3 egg yolks
1/4 cup sugar
2 spoons cocoa powder
1 tablespoon flour
Cornstarch to thicken

Heat the milk gently, and add chocolate, stirring to melt into a rich, almost steaming chocolate milk.

Whisk egg yolks, flour, sugar, cocoa and a few spoons of cornstarch into a smooth mixture.

Whisk egg yolks, flour, sugar, cocoa and a few spoons of cornstarch into a smooth mixture.

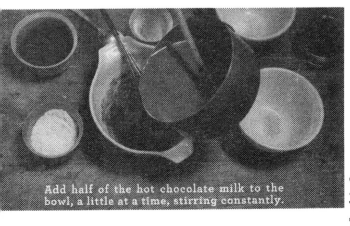

Add half of the hot chocolate milk to the bowl, a little at a time, stirring constantly.

Then add this mixture back into the rest of the hot milk, stirring over gentle heat for a few minutes until the mixture thickens to a custard.

Remove from heat and chill.

Once cooled, spoon the chocolate creme into a pastry bag and pipe into the large and medium pastry balls.

III - THE DECORATION

Prepare a glaze of of confectioners sugar, a dash of vanilla and enough milk to achieve the desired consistency.

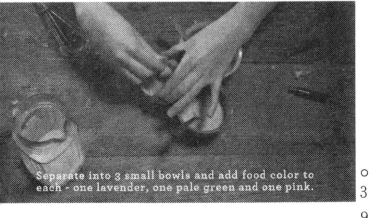

Separate into 3 small bowls and add food color to each - one lavender, one pale green and one pink.

Dip each pastry in icing (to the midline) and place it on a tray - the large pastry in lavender, the medium in pale green and the small in pink.

Decorate the balls with filigree of white chocolate as desired.

Place a dollop of icing (preferably a pale blue) atop a large pastry ball. Take a medium size ball and press it gently on the larger so it sticks in place.

Repeat with one of the small balls atop the first two.

Make a small butter cream "star" on the top and place a single cocoa bean on the star as a garnish.

Serve fresh.

You might have
to cook for 20 guys
some day.

Francis Ford Coppola
<u>Godfather</u> (1972)

Come and learn something. You might
have to cook for 20 guys some day.

You start with a little oil,
then fry some garlic.

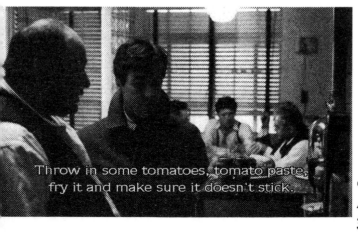

Throw in some tomatoes, tomato paste,
fry it and make sure it doesn't stick.

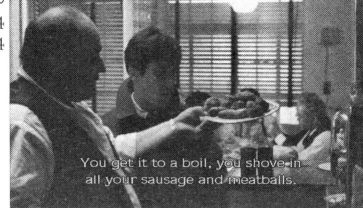

You get it to a boil, you shove in all your sausage and meatballs.

Add a little bit of wine.

And a little bit of sugar. That's my trick.

[Tennis racket
potato masher]

Jeremiah Chechik
<u>Benny and Joon</u> (1993)

[Fried egg on bread]

Hayao Miyazaki
Castle in The Sky (1986)

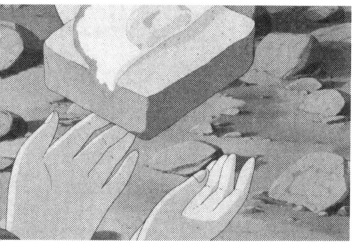

There.

Gondoa? That's so far north.

[Ale Bread]

Gabriel Axel
<u>Babette's Feast</u> (1987)

Bread

You soak it in water.

A little ale.

Then like this
through a... "sieve."

- *Tamis.*
- Yes, through a *tamis.*

Ale-and-bread soup.

- It must cook for one hour.
- Cook.

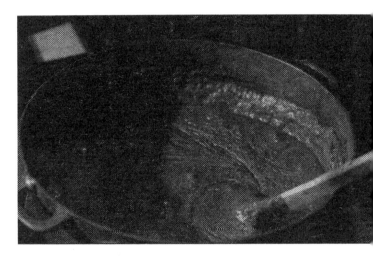

[Poached eggs]

Nora Ephron
<u>Julie and Julia</u> (2009)

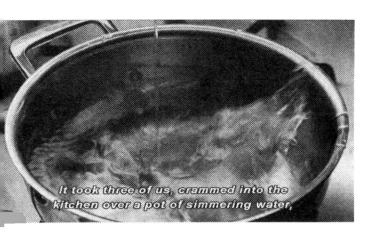

It took three of us, crammed into the kitchen over a pot of simmering water,

I had this notion, God knows why, that poaching eggs would be simple.

"Immediately and gently push the white over the yolk with a wooden spoon

"for two to three seconds." Immediately.

Disgusting.

[Mandu]

Park Chul-soo
<u>301/302</u> (1995)

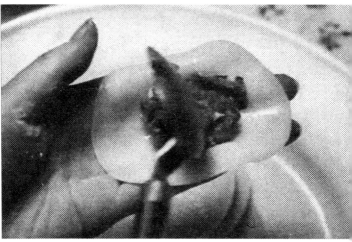

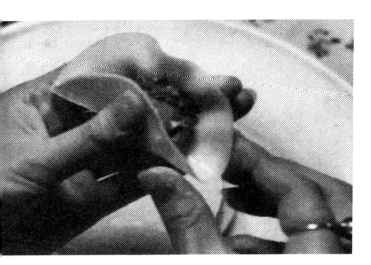

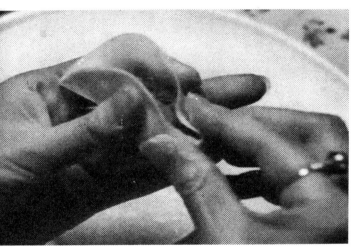

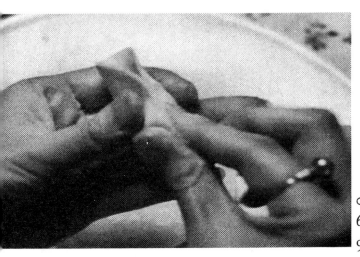

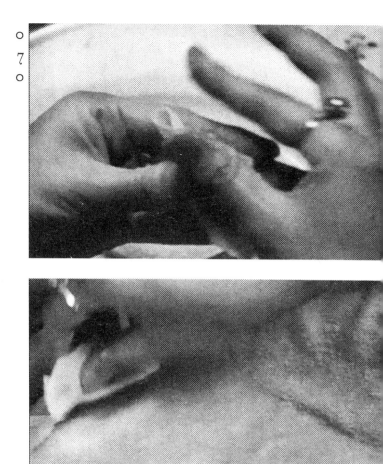

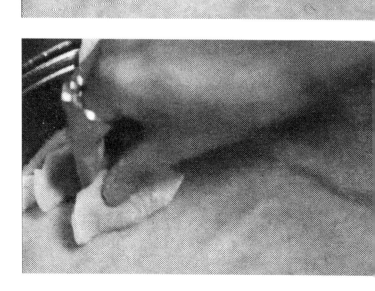

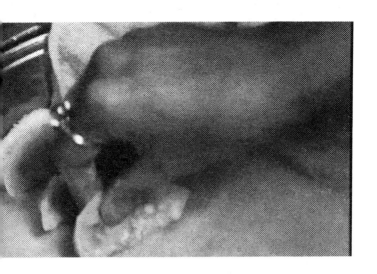

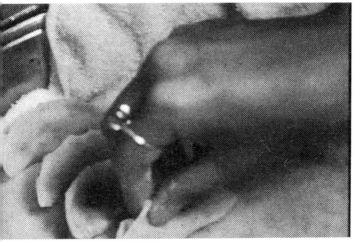

[Bossam]

Park Chul-soo
<u>3o1/3o2</u> (1995)

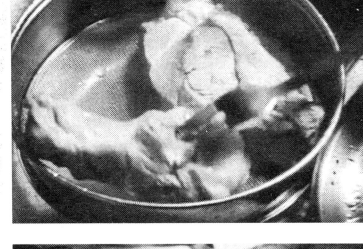

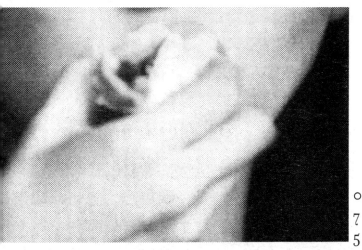

[Pickled Pond Loach]

Park Chul-soo
<u>301/302</u> (1995)

[Lobster with rock shrimp in Champagne-shallot sauce with vanilla bean and mint, served with deep-fried spaghetti and a garnish of salmon roe and wasabi-infused tobiko caviar]

Bob Giraldi
<u>Dinner Rush</u> (2000)

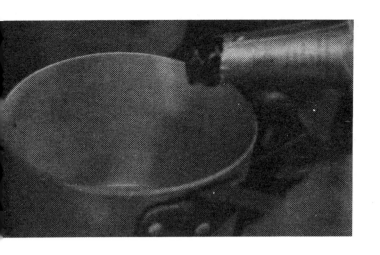

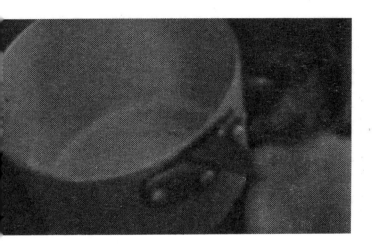

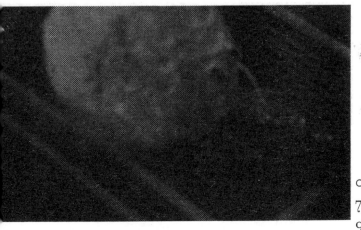

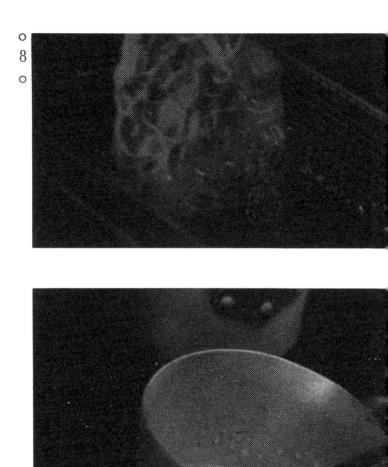

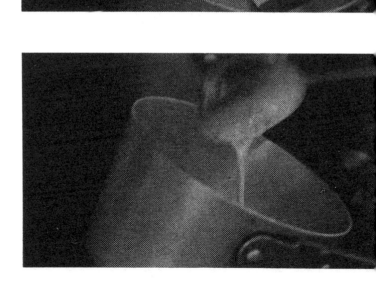

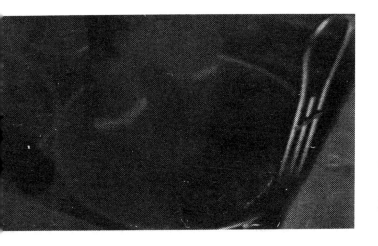

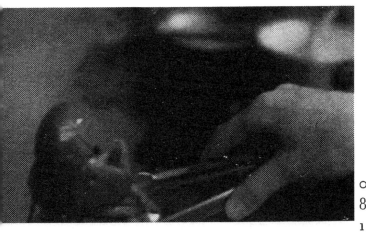

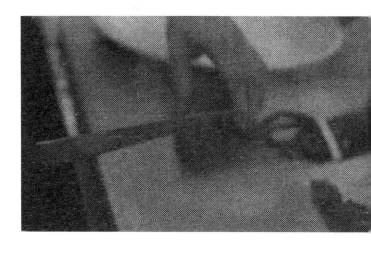

-"La bistecca alla fiorentina"...
-Tillträde förbjudet. Stick!

- What about the sauce?
- Hang on.

I'll get it ready now just in case.

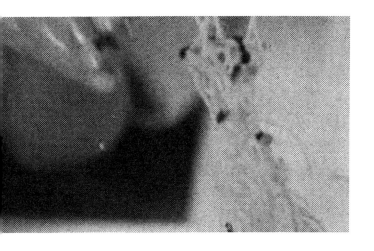

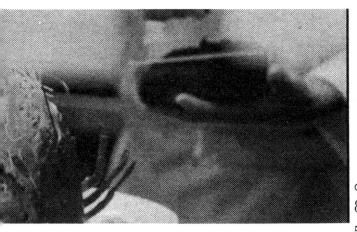

Shrimp fork, salad
fork, dinner fork.

Garry Marshall
<u>Pretty Woman</u> (1990)

Good. Elbows off the table.
Don't slouch.

Shrimp fork, salad fork, dinner fork.

I definitely have the salad fork.
The rest of the silverware
is a little confusing.

[Jiaozi]

Ang Lee
<u>Eat Drink Man Woman</u> (1994)

作曲： MADER

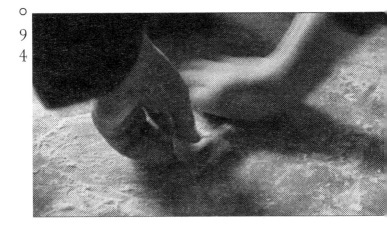

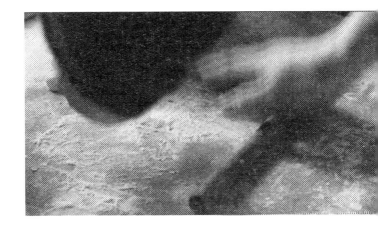

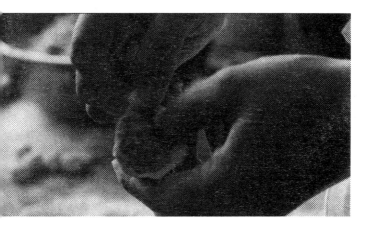

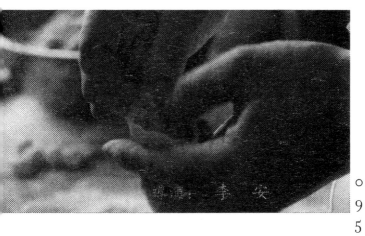

導演 李 安
Not yet?

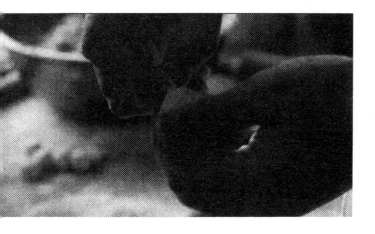

[Onigiri]

Naoko Ogigami
<u>Kamone Diner</u> (2006)

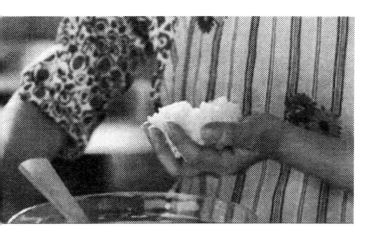

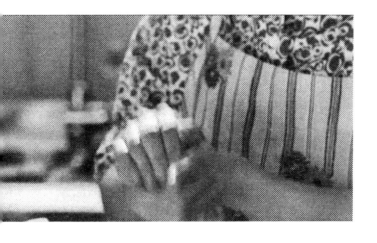

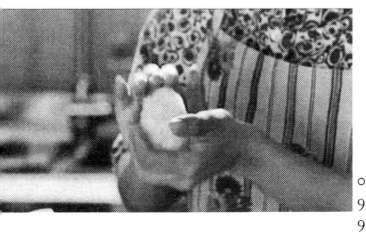

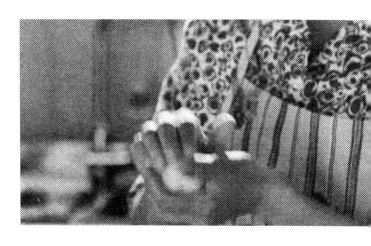

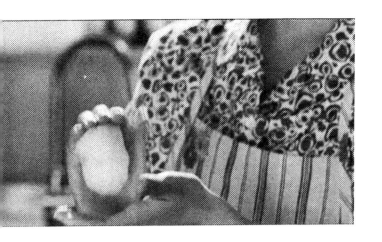

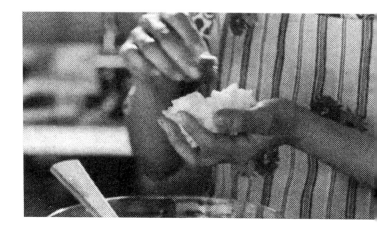

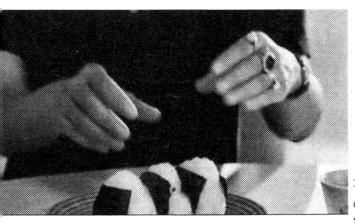

[Harkonnen Juice]

David Lynch
<u>Dune</u> (1984)

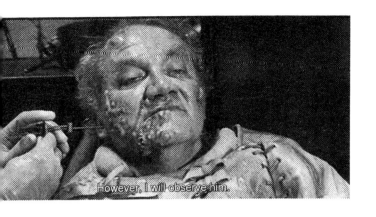

However, I will observe him.

your son will be proved
to be a living human being

or he will be a dead animal.

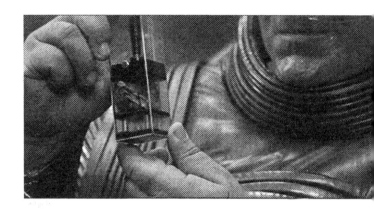

Both food and life
require salt in order
to be tastier.

Tassos Boulmetis
<u>A touche of spice</u> (2003)

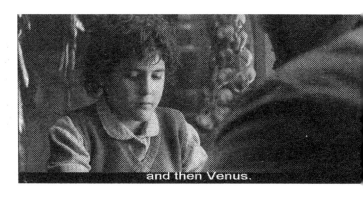

Cinnamon...

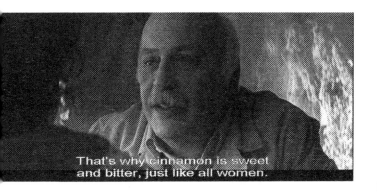

That's why cinnamon is sweet
and bitter, just like all women.

That's why cinnamon is sweet
and bitter, just like all women.

Food...

-And what makes food tastier?
-Salt...

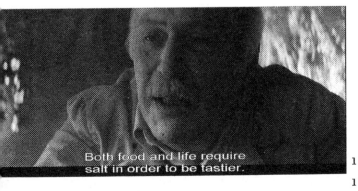

Both food and life require
salt in order to be tastier.

[Kimchi competition]

Jeon Yun-Su
<u>Le Grand Chef</u> (2007)

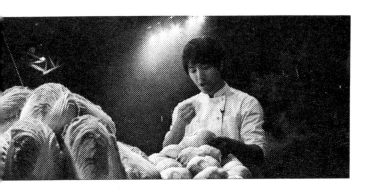

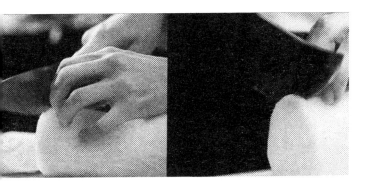

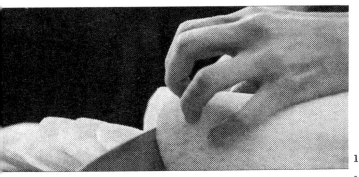

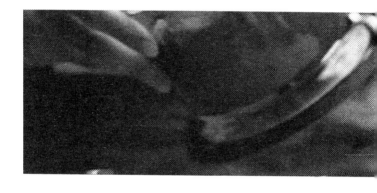

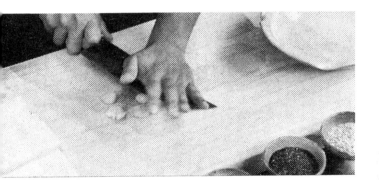

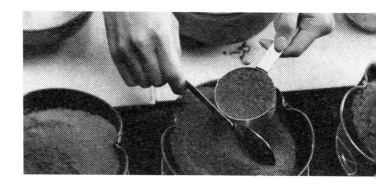

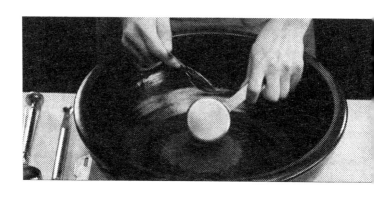

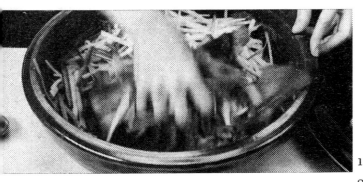

What's in the gazpacho?

Pedro Almodóvar
<u>Women on The Verge of</u>
<u>a Nervous Breakdown</u> (1988)

Chief, this stuff has been spiked.

What's in the gazpacho?

Tomatoes, cucumbers...

Don't crowd the
mushrooms,
otherwise they won't
brown.

Nora Ephron
Julie and Julia (2009)

But then I came home and cooked chicken
with cream, mushrooms and port,

and it was total bliss.

and it was total bliss.

I had been cooking mushrooms
the wrong way my entire life.

August 24th, day eleven. 353 days to go. A
horrible day at work. An old grandma who
looked as if she wouldn't harm a fly called me
a pencil pushing capitalist dupe... But then I
came home and cooked chicken with cream,
mushrooms, and port, and it was total bliss.

Here's the big news. I had been cooking
mushrooms the wrong way my entire life. Don't
crowd the mushrooms. Otherwise th|

Don't crowd the mushrooms,
otherwise they won't brown.

No oil. That's for
crap spaghetti …
Now I leave the garlic
until the spaghetti's
almost done.

Marcos Jorge
Estômago — A gastronomic Story
(2007)

The water must be boiling by now.

Let's go, Nonato.

Get the salt.

Now, stir it in.

And wait for it to cook.

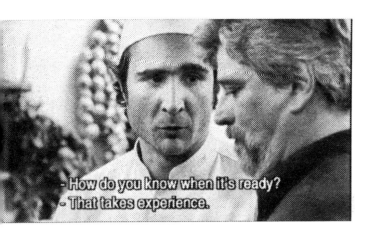

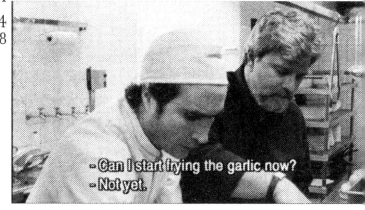

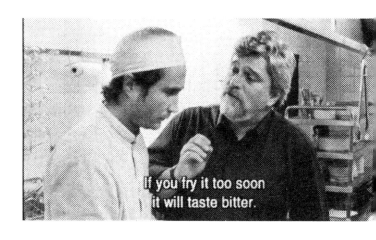

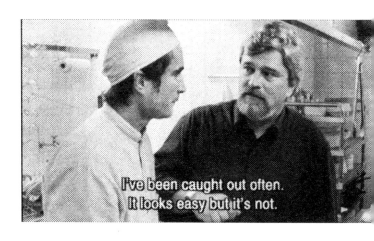

Now I leave the garlic
until the spaghetti's almost done.

- Simple things are the trickiest.
- More room for error, right?

People think they're easy
but they're not.

Obento

Hayao Miyazaki
<u>My Neighbour Totoro</u> (1988)

Sorry, I overslept again...

It's burning!

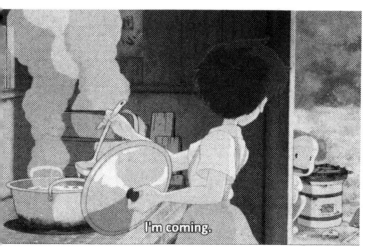

I'm coming.

Here, this is yours, Mei.

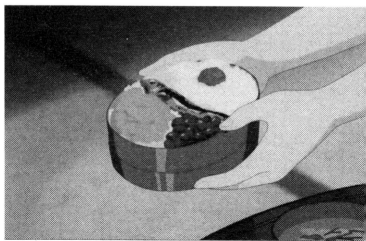

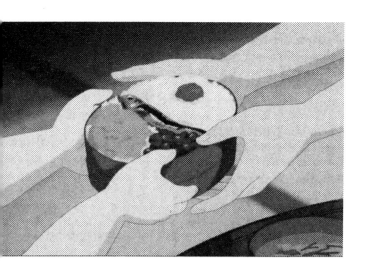

First published in the UK by Hato Press, 2016
6a Scawfell Street
London E2 8NG
hatopress.net

ISBN 978-1-910239-26-1
Printed as a run of 400
Designed by Hato
Edited by Hato and others
Printed by Hato Press

Texts, images and film stills copyright of the directors
and publishers
Typeface designed by Hato

Copies of this publication have been donated to the following UK
libraries and universities as a teaching and research resource for the
declared studies: London College of Communication; Royal College
of Art; Brighton College; Queen Margaret University; University of West
London. If you feel your library will benefit from an edition, please
contact the publishers.